I CAN BE AN

ASTRONAUT

By June Behrens

Prepared under the direction of Robert Hillerich, Ph.D.

CHILDRENS PRESS ™

CHICAGO

Library of Congress Cataloging in Publication Data

Behrens, June.
  I can be an astronaut.

  Summary: Explains the training astronauts go
through before they make their space flights.
  1. Astronautics—Vocational guidance—
Juvenile literature. [1. Astronauts.   2. Occupations]
I. Title.   II. Title: Astronaut.
TL793.B38   1984   629.45'0023   84-7601
ISBN 0-516-01837-X

PICTURE DICTIONARY

space shuttle

team

astronauts

lift-off

scientist

computer

engineer
mathematician

simulator

college

experiment

doctor

pilot

payload

spacecraft

earth

satellite

space city

orbit

Astronaut means
"sailor among the stars."
Astronauts travel in
space.

astronauts

Have you ever
watched the space
shuttle lift-off? Have

space
shuttle

lift-off

you ever wondered
what it was like? Would
you like to be an
astronaut?

Johnson Space Center, Houston, Texas

Astronauts go to school. They study at the Johnson Space Center in Houston, Texas. The school is run by NASA. NASA is the National Aeronautics and Space Administration. NASA looks for special people to travel in space.

From left to right: Calvin Burch (chief of launch operations), Dale Gardner, Dan Brandenstein, William Thornton, Guion Bluford, Richard Truly, and Larry Summers

Many people want to be astronauts. But only a few are picked.

NASA needs people who are in good health. They want people who can work together. They look for the best.

Major Frederick D. Gregory (in the pilot's seat) was the first black pilot-astronaut

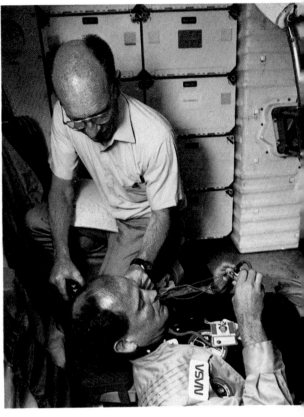

Astronauts William E. Thornton (kneeling) and Norman E. Thagard

All new astronauts have gone to college. Some are scientists or doctors. Others are engineers. Many are jet pilots.

college

scientist

engineer

doctor

pilot

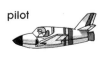

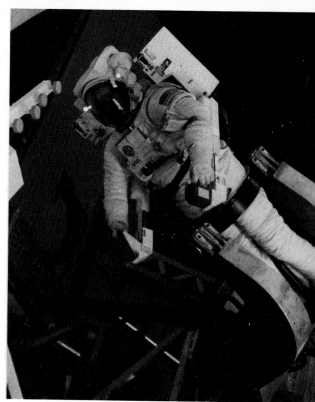

Left: New astronauts in classroom
Right: James D. van Hoften's space suit and power pack will let him move freely outside the space shuttle.

At school, new astronauts learn about space travel. They learn how the space shuttle works. They are trained to do special work in space. If something

goes wrong, they know
what to do.

Some of the teachers
were once astronauts.
They tell the new
astronauts what it is like
in space.

Scientist-astronaut Anna L. Fisher inside a simulator

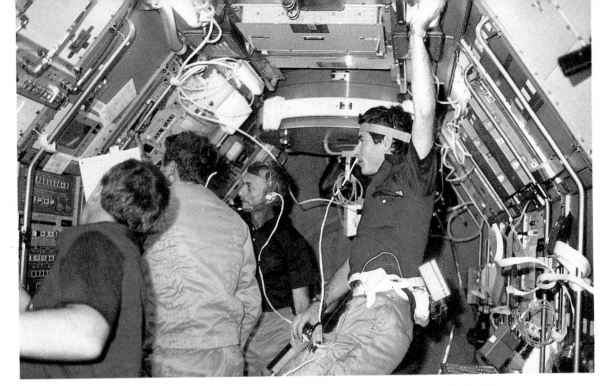

Left to right: Robert Parker, Byron K. Lichtenberg, Owen K. Garriott, and Ulf Merbold went into space in the space shuttle.

New astronauts practice in models called simulators. The model works like a spacecraft in space. Riding in the simulator is like taking a real space flight.

simulator

spacecraft

Left to right: Norman E. Thagard, Robert L. Crippen, Frederick H. Hauck, Sally K. Ride, and John M. Fabian

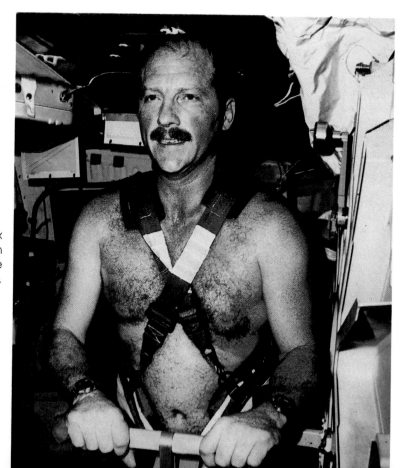

Astronaut Frederick H. Hauck works out on an exercise machine in space.

Space shuttle *Columbia* lands.

NASA teaches each new astronaut a special job. Some learn how to pilot the spacecraft. Pilots are at the controls at lift-off, in orbit, and during landing.

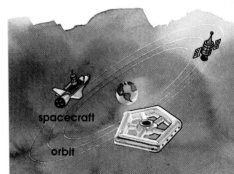

spacecraft

orbit

Astronaut Ronald E. McNair

Satellite is launched from the space shuttle.

Astronaut-pilot Frederick D. Gregory

Other astronauts learn to do special things. They do experiments in space. They might put satellites in orbit. Sometimes they work with special machines.

experiment

satellite

Space shuttle *Challenger* in orbit around the earth
with its cargo bay open

The spacecraft carries
a payload into space.
A payload is the cargo.

This robot arm (top), made in Canada, is used to put satellites into space. It also is used to grab satellites and bring them into the space shuttle to be fixed.

A payload might be a satellite. It might be other machines. Some astronauts are payload specialists. They know all about their payload.

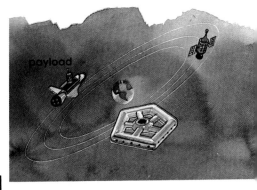

payload

Astronauts John W. Young (above) and Anna L. Fisher (below) learn to work in space suits.

Astronaut-scientist Sally K. Ride (at right) learns to parachute.

Learning to be an
astronaut is hard work.
New astronauts must
stay healthy and strong.
They must learn to do
many different things.

Clockwise: John W. Young (at top), Ulf Merbold, Owen K. Garriott, Brewster H. Shaw, Jr., Byron K. Lichtenberg, and Robert Parker were a team.

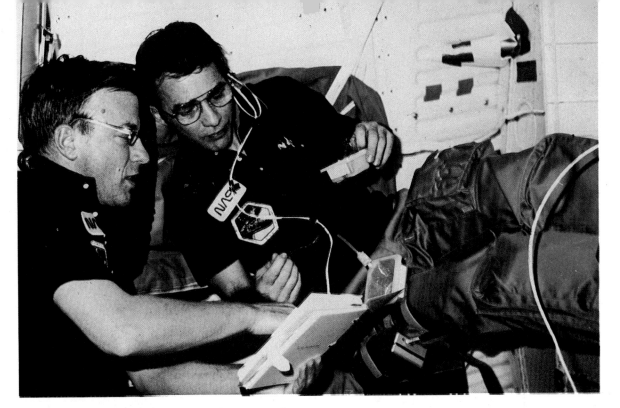

Astronauts Paul J. Weitz and Donald H. Peterson

After training, astronauts are picked for a space flight. They train as a team. The pilot, mission specialists, and payload specialists work together. They get ready for that big day.

team

Above: Mission Control Room at the Johnson Space Center, Houston, Texas

Below from left to right: Jerry C. Bostick, Daniel C. Germany, Hans Mark, and Milton A. Silveira at mission control.

During the space flight, the astronauts talk to NASA. They tell workers at NASA what they see. They explain how they feel. Workers and computers at NASA make sure the space flight is safe.

computer

One day space travel
will be part of our daily
lives. Astronauts will
build cities in space.
People will live and
work there. You may live
in space some day.

Astronaut Bruce McCandless, II outside the space shuttle near the robot arm.

Spacecraft will travel between earth and space cities. They will carry people and cargo. Many more astronauts will be needed then.

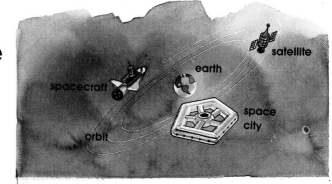

Space shuttle and its rockets before lift-off

People love to see astronauts in person. This parade was given for the astronauts who went to the moon.

Now you know what astronauts do. They work hard in school. They learn all about space travel. Astronauts have exciting jobs.

Would you like to be an astronaut?

WORDS YOU SHOULD KNOW

astronaut (AS • truh • nawt)—someone who trains to fly on spacecraft

cargo (KAR • goh)—goods that are carried by a truck, train, ship, airplane, or spacecraft

college (KAHL • ij)—a school for higher learning that follows high school

computer (kum • PYU • ter)—a machine that can work out problems when it is given facts

control (kun • TROHL)—something that makes a machine act in a certain way

daily (DAY • lee)—taking place every day

engineer (en • juh • NEER)—a person who plans and builds things such as machines, roads, and bridges

experiment (ek • SPAIR • uh • ment)—a way of finding out if something works and how it works

flight (FLYT)—a trip in an airplane or a spacecraft

healthy (HELTH • ee)—having good health

mission (MISH • un)—a trip to carry out special work

model (MAHD • il)—a small copy that is just like the real thing

orbit (OR • bit)—the path that one body in space follows around another. A spacecraft makes an orbit around the earth.

payload (PAY • lode)—the load carried. In a spacecraft the payload may be things for experiments, cargo, or astronauts.

pilot (PY • let)—a person who handles the controls of an airplane or spacecraft

sailor (SAY • ler)—a person who handles or sails on a ship of some kind

satellite (SAT • el • ite)—an object that orbits around the earth or some other body in space. Man-made satellites are sent into orbit from spacecraft.

scientist (SY • en • tist)—a person who has special training in a field that has to do with such things as people, plants, animals, the earth, and space

shuttle (SHUT • il)—a bus, train, airplane, or spacecraft that goes back and forth between two places

simulator (SIM • yuh • lay • ter)—a practice machine or room that lets people find out exactly what will happen when they use the real thing. Astronauts practice in simulators to learn what will happen in space.

space (SPAISS)—what is farther on past the air that is around the earth

spacecraft (SPAISS • kraft)—a machine that flies in outer space

specialist (SPESH • uh • list)—a person who works at one special kind of job or part of a job

travel (TRAV • il)—to go from one place to another

INDEX

PHOTO CREDITS

NASA (National Aeronautics and Space Administration)—cover, 4, 6, 8, 9, 10, 11, 12, 13, 14, 15, 16, 17, 18, 19, 20, 21, 22, 23, 24, 26, 27

Hillstrom Stock Photos: © Journalism Services—28; © Brooks & Van Kirk—29

Tom Dunnington—2-3

About the Author

JUNE BEHRENS has written more that fifty books, plays, and filmstrips for young people, touching on all subject areas of the school curriculum. Mrs. Behrens has for many years been an educator in one of California's largest public school systems. She is a graduate of the University of California at Santa Barbara and has a Master's degree from the University of Southern California. Mrs. Behrens is listed in *Who's Who of American Women*. She is a recipient of the Distinguished Alumni Award from the University of California for her contributions in the field of education. She and her husband live in Rancho Palos Verdes, a southern California suburb.